I0510521

THIS NOTEBOOK BELONGS TO

____

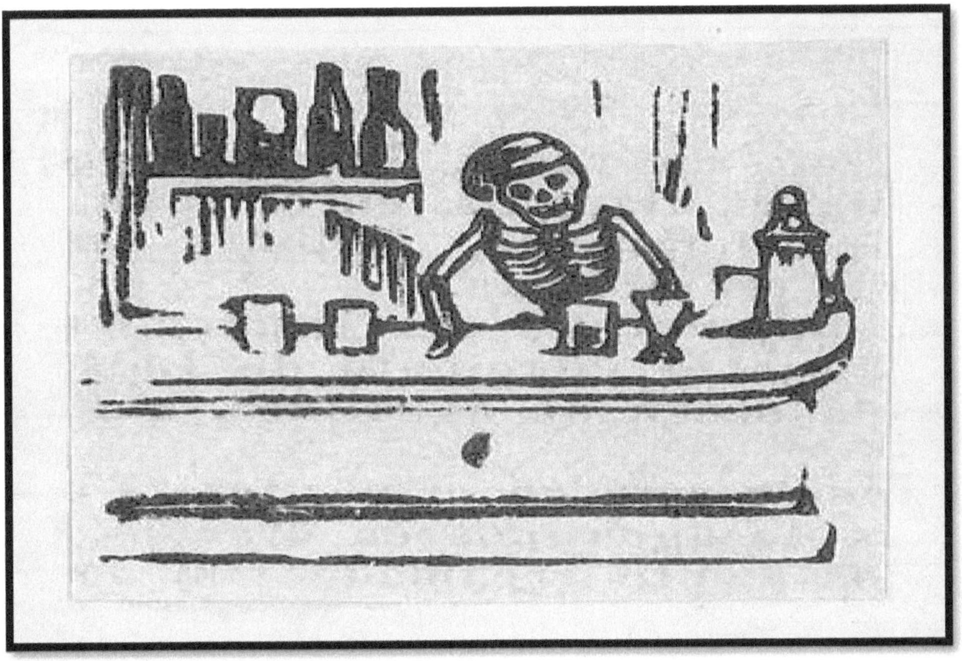

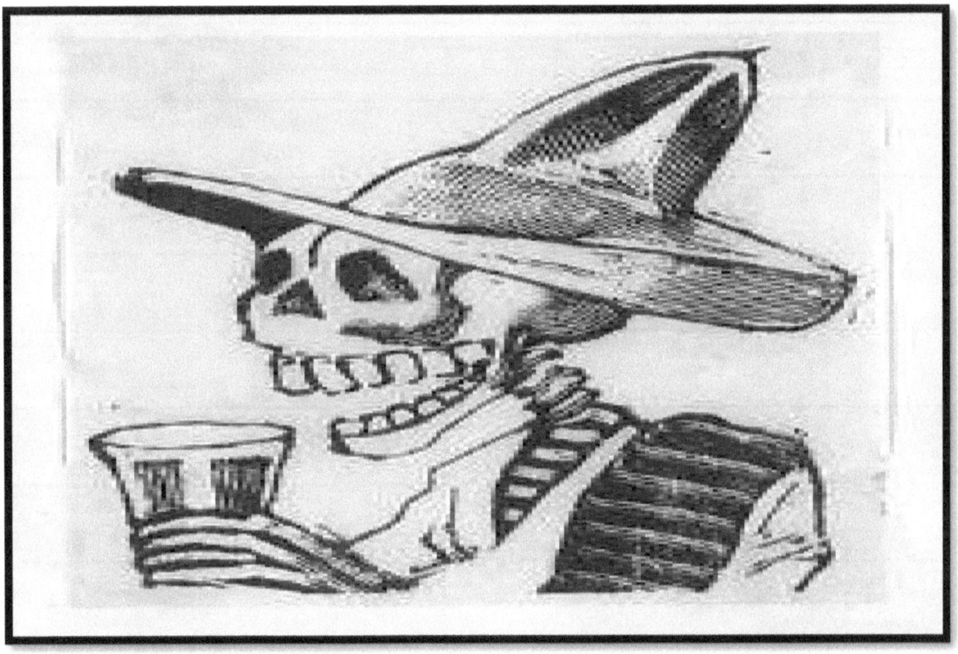

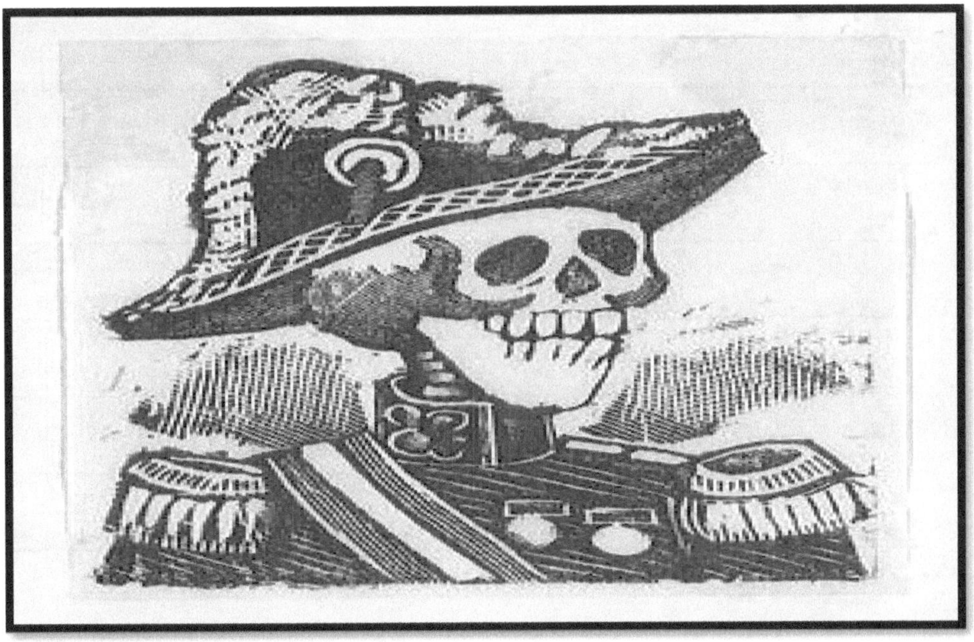

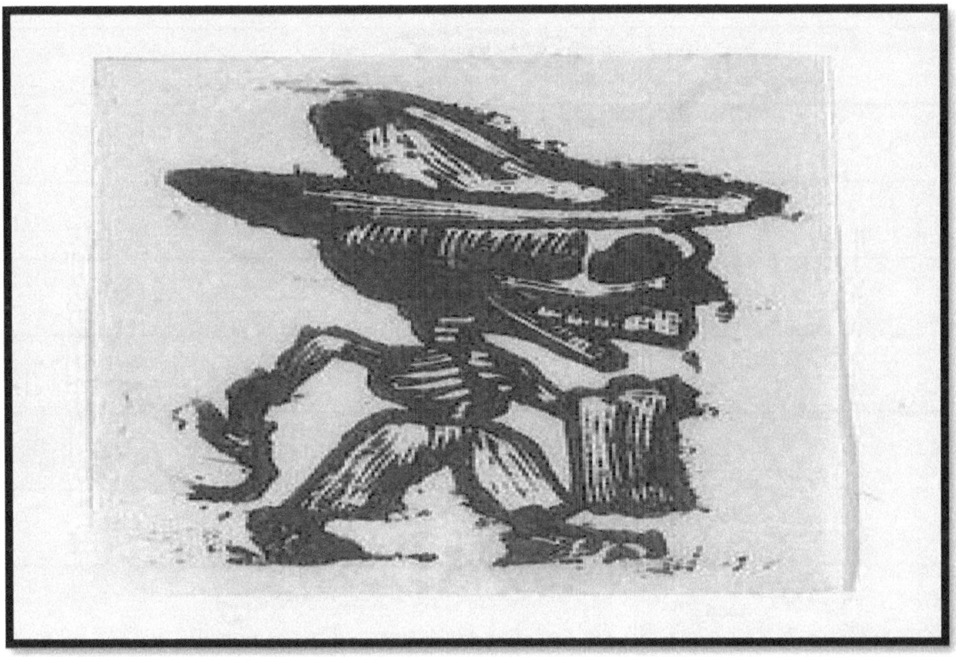

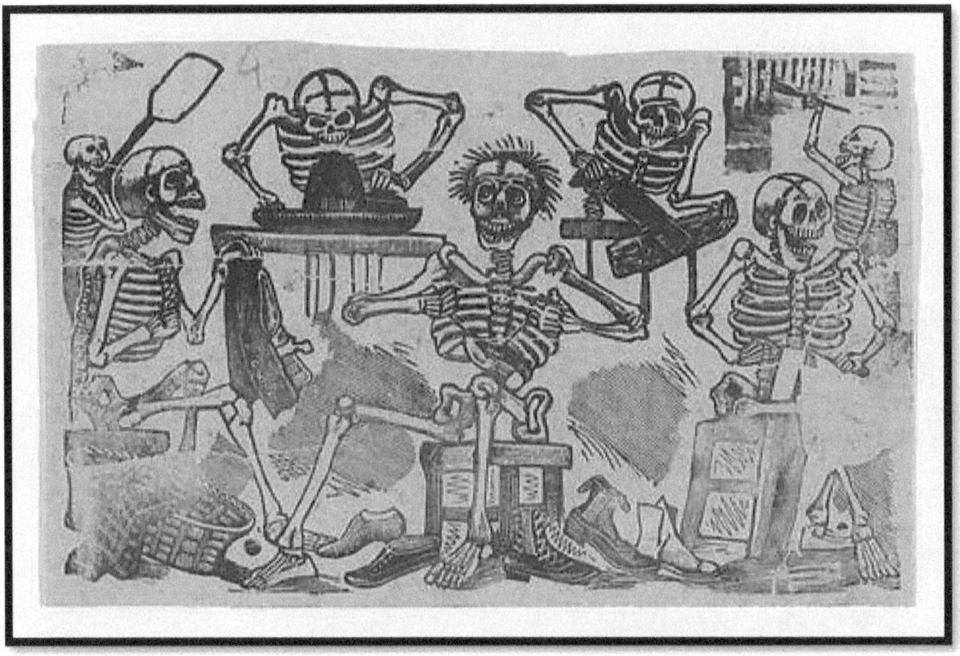

www.ingramcontent.com/pod-product-compliance
Lightning Source LLC
Chambersburg PA
CBHW030946240526
45463CB00016B/1972
9781697541052